QUEEN OF DARKNESS

Grateful acknowledgment is made to *American Report* for "Queen of Darkness" and "Alone"; *Aphra* for "We Are"; *Arion's Dolphin* for "A Visit to My Astrologer" and "The Death of a Revolutionary"; *Atlantic Monthly* for "X-Ray" and "Room 635, Wing B"; *Blacksmith Anthology* for "On Refusing Your Invitation to Come to Dinner"; *Boston Phoenix* for "Marriage"; *Film Library Quarterly* for "Garbo"; *Harvard Crimson* for "The God in Us Wishes to Live"; *Kayak* for "Language Is the Survival of the Race," "Whales Sing," "Virgo," and "Life in Fat City"; *Maio* for "The Bird," "Barcelona," and "Life and Death of Hero Stick"; *Ms* for "At the Church of the Panagia Kera (All Holy Lady)"; *Partisan Review* for "The Solitary One" and "She Comes to Him on Their Anniversary"; *Pulp* for "Your Mouth"; *The Real Paper* for "Birthday Poem"; *Sailing the Road Clear* for "Madam Carnelia Does Solemnly Swear to Fulfill Every Claim She Makes," "Danae at the Hermitage," "From Her Cave," "Persephone Departs," and "She Paints,"; *Small Moon* for "Little Devil" and "Greek Song"; *Softball* for "Still Life, Biafra"; *Women/Poems III* for "Anne's Wedding"; *Women/Poems IV* for "Initiation."

Queen
of
Darkness

CELIA GILBERT

THE VIKING PRESS NEW YORK

Library of Congress Cataloging in Publication Data
Gilbert, Celia, 1932–
Queen of darkness.
I. Title.
PS3557.I335Q4   811'.5'4   76-54855
ISBN 0-670-58395-2

Printed in the United States of America
Set in IBM Journal

For Jean Boudin

CONTENTS

QUEEN OF DARKNESS

THE BIRD

It was a bird
I had forgot to give drink,
wearied, the head was slipping
down to death and then
I brought it water in
a bowl, its eye
opened on me it
became a man,
who would not remember,
being bird,
though I spoke of this event,
strange,
many times.

LANGUAGE IS THE SURVIVAL
OF THE RACE

Dawn came in the foreign capital.
After a night of love
The travelers awoke refreshed.
"Yours is the victory," she said to him,
Or, "you win," in the vernacular.
Check one: the birds—(squeak), (shriek), (twitter), (moan).
When the park was unwrapped, it revealed
Four drunks, eight benches, one statue, and twelve trees.
Made in Finland was stamped at the base.
They were enchanted.
They had never seen anything so real.
Real broken glass. "Beer bottles, I think," said brother.
"Listen," said the mother, "you can hear something,"
It was the sound of motor bikes
And the heavy breathing of foreigners in the hotel.
The Finnish language has fourteen case endings for nouns.
The abessive is my favorite case.
Travel is broadening.
We are making love like Finns.
Professor Chomsky, the linguist, would cite the preceding
Statement as one of obscure difficulty.
But a child could understand it.
Have we proved the theory of a Universal Human Grammar?
Everyone we know today is an astronaut.
It is a very popular profession
If you like machines.
Mars moved rapidly through the clear sky last night.

The Baltic is a sweet sea; the shipworm
Cannot survive in its waters.
"In our country," we explained slowly, "everything
Perishes quickly."
The students seemed to comprehend.
"We will never do last night again," he said,
"But perhaps we will do it better..."
She shuddered, with pleasure.
"I do not know. Perhaps."

WHALES SING

Whales sing.
Learning this, oh,
Another time we
Would have said,
Praise Him.

Now, praise them,
Our milk brothers, hunted,
As we are hunted,
Makers of songs,
A dying race.

They fashion for the few
Who lie, vast
And distant, listening
For one another,
A music, complex

Exalted. Their hoots
And echoes sound
The deepest registers
Of loneliness,
And love:
A *vox humana*
On the ocean's
Windy reed.

BARCELONA

Dreaming again of Barcelona.
Do you remember going where

We didn't want to go
In order to stay where we needed to?

"Your papers," they said.
"Numbers must be put in order."

So we went. Over
The Pyrenees the sound of running

Water, ringing against the sharp sky.
Then out of that blue

Arriving dirty on the hot
Slow train, the benches

In the third class plain
As pine coffins and the passengers

With their hands folded
Eyes open, silent. We can't speak.

We don't know the language.
Like a joke, at first, but

There's no asking why the haystacks
Huddle like sick brown monkeys

Watching, and the earth
Is a soiled remnant.

When the train lies down
The passengers go up in smoke.

We sparrow out, hungry
Wary, looking over the hedges

At the people gorging:
Sweating tons of grease.

Setting down the plates
The waiter's hands clack,

Eyes of yellow marble,
Teeth of famished dogs.

The sailors are squinting
At me. Fat girl with

Two men in turtlenecks.
The harbor is a cracked canvas:

One schooner under a wormy moon.
Rats are boarding. We could

Sail off to golden Peru.
But we get lost in the back alley

Where a caped man, holding a lantern
Comes jangling keys

"All is well," he creaks. We run
Upstairs into a high room.

Under a light bulb—a woman
Forges identities. Points us

To a partition.
All night, whispers, business.

We lie fearful, but
Fail to stay awake.

The streetcars screech at dawn.
At the wharf, the ship is gone.

Soldiers are everywhere:
Black hats, black boots, red lips.

We are nothing,
Lonelier than the poor.

Here's the cathedral, remarkable
As a saint's knuckle.

And the day burns on
Cooking the city in benzine.

At dusk a man settles in the park,
Mumbles, fires his finger

Ratatat into the rising moon.
A gift of tongues.

"The general kills the Basques."
We understand. He laughs.

We laugh. We hold a wake,
Swearing not to sleep this night.

In a dive, drinking, faces
Sly round the eyes, stare at us.

Corpulent men, holding their women,
Stab by our table, smiles shut.

Shivering on a bench till dawn,
We take the first train out.

Noon on the border the guards
Are clicking like metronomes

Timing our fears. We go
Three in a row. A game

Of boxes, naughts, and crosses.
We return to the Tricolor

Like ghosts raised up
By the Custom's wink and shrug.

MARRIAGE

we merfolk
strain for air
the pure empyrean...

home: under the rotting wood
under the jetty, we float
in and out.

the young are gone,
gone to Frau Holle, land
of unwanted children.

time now, knives sharp, we begin
the climb from darkness
on to lesser darkness.

on to the rocks
mussel-scarred blue-black.
then higher, dryer

where the locust pods hiss
at our feet; nuts
fist their meats.

above the mountains
the night is cutting
a new moon: old enigma.

THE GOD IN US WISHES TO LIVE

I

Beautiful goldfish,
eyes upon wide this world, our visitor
without a claw,
only a reflex of love,
a fist to close on a finger
that isn't there,
telling me you need Yoga
because Daddy never noticed.

At ten you were a sugar freak.
At fifteen your mother starved you
because your breasts were too big.
Now you fast and love the Swami,
peck at fruits, grains,
hungry all the time.

The body hangs by its feet weightless
in the headstand, spirals in the Twist,
opens into the Lotus, Cobra, Plough,
Locust, Bow, Bridge;
a spectacular view of the labial crest
in the shoulder stand.

Meditate on a point between the eyes,
candle flame, or rose,
to reach

the wavering self: a handful of bone,
the blind unwinking navel.

Holding the soles of the feet
transmits
a pleasurable warmth
up through the body.

II

Somewhere in darkened rooms women lie
gnarled as roots.
The doctors whisper, "Sigh, sigh,"
and they sigh.
"Breathe, breathe,"
and they breathe. Over and over.
Needles pricking the old grooves. Scream!
Uncoil. "Give it to me, give it to me.
Give." Veins on the neck stand
thick as chains. Rings throttling fingers,
gold watches tick on swollen wrists.
The spine arches
releasing tears.
"Good," whisper the doctors,
"you're getting there."

Where?
Back to the mouthing
of the warm wet eye?
Where did they put the child
who wanted to suck her thumb
who sucked sheets and socks and humiliation
when they put the bitter alum on her fingers?

III

Shattered, put together,
you are here,
standing on your head,
passed through the hands
of many men, like water,
like Rama's Sita,
proving her innocence
in the fire.
Your lungs gnaw air
you are filled, emptied, filled

and you move off
Taos, Nepal, Bay City, Windy City,
heading east by west, with the others,
looking for a place.

"MADAM CARNELIA DOES SOLEMNLY SWEAR
TO FULFILL EVERY CLAIM SHE MAKES"

Madam Carnelia in the dark room the green room.
Madam Carnelia where the scented candle burns drugged white.
Madam Carnelia the kitchen curtains close their eyes.
Madam Carnelia the plastic begonias, are they eternal?
Madam Carnelia your fingers are swollen with power to heal.
Madam Carnelia the neighbors slam the doors on you.
Madam Carnelia I smell you, the web of your flesh.
Madam Carnelia what lies down in the cave of your mouth?
Madam Carnelia the black of your skin is my sorrow.
Madam Carnelia the tips of your fingers are rosebuds.
Madam Carnelia between your thighs your cunt is a river.
Madam Carnelia your ears grow like mushrooms.
Madam Carnelia you are the one who must hear the truth.
Madam Carnelia I tremble at the hairs on your lip.
Madam Carnelia whose plates are there in the sink? whose cups?
Madam Carnelia you are grains of sand, you are honey in a spoon.
Madam Carnelia you are a ferris wheel, you are a smooth stone.
Madam Carnelia your voice is a rope in a well.
Madam Carnelia seeing the roads with your nose.
Madam Carnelia my wife is losing her breast.
Madam Carnelia I am the dog meat on the griddle I clean.
Madam Carnelia my veins hang out of my ass.
Madam Carnelia the kid is sick, he wets the bed, he is ten.
Madam Carnelia cut the cards find the way where is the door?
Madam Carnelia who is working this evil this life?
Madam Carnelia conceal nothing, take from me sorrow & darkness.
Madam Carnelia here is my money, you smile; smile, bless my money.

WE ARE

You are
the kitchen sink
take everything
fast as I can.
and I

am the telephone
ear ear
breathe me
ring ring.
You are

the disposal
oh what small hammers
go round and round
in you.
And I

am the Waring Blendor
weary little knives
chop chop
make it so's we can
drink it.
You are

the dryer
arid arguments

take the wet
out of my blankets.
And I

am the washing machine
pretending to clean
those stains
but secretly fixing
them in forever.
You are

the air conditioner
endlessly
pumping dead air
into the room.
And I

am the vacuum
sucking the dust up
weaving it into your filters.
You are

the self-defrost
freezer
morgue of the family cut-rate feasts.
And I

am the electric
self-cleaning oven
ready to bake
plastic children.
You are

Daddy Warbucks
in a suit of green
General Motors
Doctor Spock
Uncle Tom.
And I

am Betty Crocker
Aunt Jemima
Mrs. America
M.M. at the end of her dream
the Candidate's Wife,
eyeballs blue rinsed
argo-starched.
We have

a sixty-day service
guarantee.

THE WIDOWER

In a house of shadows
he sits
on chairs handpainted by the first.
He cooks with ritual vessels
of the second.
They left their stuff
in the closet
and came back, clouds.

One sits at his right hand.
One sits at his left hand.
Hard to say whose death
was the bigger victory.
As printers justify a line,
their going corrected
an old error.

He's a big bruiser with
a delicate mind and
he knows how to
pick his ladies:
they give way, give way.

Sole survivor, he has inherited the property:
the bees' industry,
the gossip of the trees.
He's on to the birds' jargon,

can hear the grass grow,
drink the ocean dry,
eat and never be satisfied.

He's a legend in these parts,
a warlock, some say.
Men admire the blond and brunette
scalps he sports
and his guts, to live
in *that* house;
but women, carrying, feel the fetus
quiver
when he walks down the lane
listening to twin whispers,
"You loved me best."
"Me best."

Together, the rivals, blot his ink, burn his toast,
spill the milk weeping
and make the fire smoke, but worst
they mimic his mother's voice,
calling him, "little mouse."
That's when he roars, "Women, you'll see
I can kill, more than twice..."
He's looking for a new one now.
His tastes run that way.

GARBO

Her face is the moon's: far
sickle of indifference
until close and full
it breaks
over the horizon,
too sweet its slow globe of honey,

and then,
the totalitarian
locked wards
of her gaze.

THE GENIE

I have been in this bottle so long,
shoulders cramped,
eyes squinting to see
through the glass,
mantled in dust,
but,
it's the right line of work for me:
that thrill of being needed,
of gratifying your least desire.
I've been bread, I've been wine,
after dinner, night after night,
I've been your garden of earthly delight.

You do it with a rub of the hand
and a command.
I am smiles, goods, money.
I am lies, I am wise.
Always after the tricks performed,
back to the bottle,
but I'm so tired I don't mind, only
confused, a bit bewildered
after the applause and the power
to be so small and still.

But that's a genie's life
I tell myself.
This is what it's like to be a genie.

And I think how good it is
to have a master who rubs me
the right way,
because they say there are genies
unrecognized in junk yards, or
bobbing in rivers.
Days when my back aches from confinement
I remind myself
how lucky I am
to be on the shelf.

21

YOUR MOUTH

for Mme. Mandelstam

A child's mouth
Fallen into an old woman's shrug,
   Swollen like her feet.
      Mouth
Corroded by accusations
Against the double agents,
   Men in slippers,
   Men who look away from you
Repelled by that mouth
   Which spits them out.

It won't stop tasting
Forbidden words
   As you recall
The long years of posthumous living
   The frigid winters asleep
On the frozen stove.
     Under the pastoral brown
Of eyes that signal for help,
   Your mouth
     Won't surrender.
  You gnaw at its edges
    Taking it
For sustenance.

X-RAY

the bones gleam
out of the dark.
like the ghost of a fern
in stone here
are spine and ribs.

the skull
of my daughter is
a cup:
        something is drinking her life up.
there are islands shadowed
on her brain
        white tides are washing
                washing them out.

THE FIRST DAY OF DEATH

Man of Egypt
in the House of Death
this first day of death,
will you have room
for the doll,
for the many bits of small
of a small life?
Will you weave
over and over the white web
tight and perfect
as the caul,
to cradle the voyager
on her endless journey
through an airless time?

You are not the man of Egypt
in the House of Death.
Your head is not shaved in respect.
The hairs are already falling
from my head
and in every cell of my body
there is the nudity
of grief.

You are not the man of Egypt
in the House of Death.
Your feet are not bare.

They do not acknowledge
the dust.
Your hands are not held out to us,
the first day of death,
palms upwards and outwards,
so we may read your suffering
and your skill.
We cannot see your body.
It is only right
that we should see
your body...
You have none.
You are only a skull with flabby cheeks
and bits of hair glued
to your head.

The first day of death
we have given her body to the magicians.
As we talk in your house
they are taking her
piece by piece.
Are the magicians better than worms?

If we believe in the fire,
why did we not take her ourselves
and set fire to the flesh we made?
We have never smelled burning flesh.
We have never held a scalpel,
we have lived, then, in darkness
pretending it was light.
Why do we not eat her?

The first day of death
is it so unnatural to want a piece of earth
to kneel on and feel
her spirit?
We do not believe in that.
We have nothing to do with the soul.
We have nothing to do with the body.
There is no circle of mourners.
What will we do?

Let us enter the house:
the hole in our side is too large to conceal.
Let us paint our faces:
the mouths will be very red,
the eyes wreathed in blue.
Only lines on the forehead will show
where we have failed.

BIRTHDAY POEM

Alone now, and most certainly.
Alone
in a room.

Shadows spiral
in the
updraft.

The acrid sex of the tomato.
Moist pulp
swollen.

Milkweed pods still green.
Inside the seed
packed tight and wet.

Over the autumn stubble
the cow crops
in peace.

Stalks topple,
the wasp's children
eat.

She leaves him.
He leaves her.
"Used, used," they cry.

The marigolds persist,
rank suns
uneclipsed by cold.

The self I hid
so many years
alone, now, most certainly.

DANAE AT THE HERMITAGE

Danae is so surprised—or is she?
Naked, she rises from the bedclothes. Who
is there?
Why is Cupid weeping?
She is ignorant,
wise to the golden rain,
not to the coffer adrift
and rocking.
Spendthrift and then, impotent,
Zeus left a child for the tip.
But none of that is in the painting,
only her beauty and desire
caught in the light
of his largess.

Here, in Leningrad, the guide
explains these foreign
names: Danae, Zeus.
A Russian stares,
stuck in the honey
of the painted flesh, and
sees: a woman the painter knew
who loved him, this was how she leaned
and looked
hearing his step
upon the stair...

Prodigious belly.
He calculates its wealth,
imagines spending hours stroking
that pampered skin. He thinks
of his wife,
their bed's rough sheets;
how the milky summer nights spill over
their breasts;
how the long winter dark
wears them down
with its old gums.

FROM HER CAVE

A distant people wrapped in skins
come near and penetrate my room.
History,
       I've
caught up to it,
having one as you have,
and you.
That heavy book on my knees
is light now.

I put my foot on warped brick
over the elm's bony root
and walk
to your side, child, dying,
and yours, Marat, subsiding in your tub
under the bloody bubbles.
The knife is in my kitchen
and in my closet the dress I wore
the day you die.

Long before I scratched the moon on bone
I mourned what was untimely.
The tide traces a horn, the cave
a beast's curved back.
Words
rush from my throat.

VIRGO

for Kate

Hours...the short distance from school
findings: toad, red bead,
newt, quick as grass.

              Past everyone's happy ending
moving slowly, attending messages tom-tomed
by worms, reading the lives

of dogs, wet noses telling the palm.
A bag scrapes against the bricks,
bits of world cut up, pasted down:
great men, the Straits of Magellan.

              Ascending the path where
the pears rot, the blurred body
grows knowledge more distinct each day

entering this house.

THE SOLDIER

His mouth is a pink grenade,
his blue eyes catch on safety,
he watches what we're saying.

We're only sitting here
drinking tea,
what's so remarkable?

A sleep starts seeping
from his eyes
like a yellow gas.

We all fall over; his wife
his child, into a ditch.
We try to climb out.

His rifle butt,
we move back. Cry.
He shakes his head.

This is a mistake
a mistake
        mistake.

His eyes turn black.
We're out of focus.
Pieces of him are everywhere.

QUEEN OF DARKNESS

My shadow
was all that I possessed.
Did you know
when you brought me to this land
I would lose it?

The blind are happy here,
scurry along the trails, meet
forehead to forehead.
"Their eyes are false," I said.
"The bulging lens reflects
a glassy dark—
reports nothing back."
But you assured me
they see as well as you
or I.

Strange, you seemed
like everyone else
until we came here.
Now you have ceased to talk,
stroking my hips and thighs
silently, silently.

I am afraid to look
at your sleek black head,
your pinched waist. In my lap

glowing like jet, you dwindle,
but there is power in you,
while I mourn for my shadow,
speechless,
your creature.

In my room I queen it.
My abdomen grows thick
and swollen. Old women
shuffle in, bringing food.
They touch me
for good luck.
What fills me
is none of my doing.

ROOM 635, WING B

Father lay in the crib.
His eyes struggled like moths to reach the light.
His nose tunneled the dark.

The curse of life lay on the children
The curse of life lay on the wife.
They stood around the bed.

"Nurse, Nurse, get the Nurse..."

Liquid trickles from the mast;
a blood bag hangs at the feet.

"He was big enough to spank a little girl," his daughter says.
"He was big enough to eat up little boys," his sons report.
"His nice-nice was the world to me," stated his wife.

Who put this dummy here, in place
of father dear?

Room 635, Wing B.
The sky is a silent film.
The window a dead end; heat hisses
like a gas
pulling us into sleep.

Quick, quick
fetch the basin, father's sick.

"He's so big
when he fell
one arm knocked a building down.
The Rockies were his pocketcomb."

From the clouds, reproachful:
"Oh where were you? Why weren't you
here?"

"There, there,
there, there."

Uncovered, thin yellow legs.
Don't look,
Canaan was cursed.

Shh, outside the legend grows:
how prodigious the energy,
crayoned yellow sun with spikey crown.
Shh...

But what are we to do with this body?
The air leaking from it
is filling us up.

The pressure is intolerable;
we are balloning
into grown-ups;
set to drift.

Two black queens
trundle you away—

rag doll, Thunderer,
leaf.

THE CAVE AND THE FIG TREE

Come, descend the steps where the fig tree
throws its green hands to the sky.
Pass under the wrinkled arch of earth
over the slippery rubble,
silently, this is the relearning of the way.
And the women came here in their time and prayed,
bringing the little they had.
I am in you again. And you in me tremble,
fill me and wait to climb the stairs.

The sound of the cricket, mining the shadows.
Dark grips us. This is how we came,
the moisture slowly dripping,
the ferocious busyness
of the cells, the muscles' liturgy.

We pray to the mother goddess
of the pinched nose, the closed eyes,
her hands raised, fingers like ten twigs.
Light smokes at the entrance of the cave.
She whispers the final word.
You turn and turn, now there is no stopping.
The blue waits shining with its knife
to pry you out,
but this dark is with you
forever.

LIFE IN FAT CITY

The egg breaks
The womb has a good cry.
She loves her potential—
Hasn't got that much
Going for her, anyway.
Her eggs are numbered.
And she tried.
Good hostess,
She plumped the pillows,
Warmed the bed,
Laid in provisions.
"Business is bad," says the Widow.

Here comes the
Gunfighter.
He's real mean.
Couldn't care less.
He's got this here
Apparatus shoots
Silver bullets...
Plenty more where they come from.
When he swaggers by
Cocked and ready
Look out.

We know the scenario
Everybody dives for the floor.

This guy
Has got what it takes
To kill:
Unlimited supplies,
All day.

Will the Widow
Ask him
In?

A VISIT TO MY ASTROLOGER

Nothing, the stars deride.
Nothing more than I have known
seeing my hand on the table,
my face in the shop window.

If I am afflicted in Pluto,
I am exalted in Pluto
to rise earthbound, to sink skyward,
to lie along lines of waiting, barred and boxed,
O degrees that tax the power of the heart!

Head in Moon,
my soul put out in Jupiter's
leaky vessel, I navigated,
tied to the mast, ears waxed.

Yes, my Virgo darling, we'll come through.
Years, more difficult than artichokes, pile up,
at their heart, greenest plenitude.
Out there, where a voice calls *light, more light,*
holding a candle, I walk on
steadily, to the edge of the dark.

LITTLE DEVIL

Only the Pope says Satan still walks the earth,
but I have a devil, small and still,
named Leave-The-Bills-To-Me,
named Don't-Move-I'll-Do-It,
named Close-Your-Eyes-And-Let-Me-Stroke-You,
named Sleep-With-Contentment.
He is as bitter as earwax, and keeps out the noise,
He is as constant as an ice-cream cone can
never be licked down.
He is a house cat as big as an owl
with asthma.
He is a pair of silver hands.

In the morning picking roses
no thorns can hurt me.
At night I pluck my lute
effortlessly.
The devil nodding in my lap
I search for lice
and snap them with my clever fingers.

But there is being tired of devils,
yet no doctor prescribes.
There is being wearied of devils
but no mother understands.
There is wanting to get rid of the devil—
but this makes a father very angry.

There is looking around for ways to drown the devil,
to shoot the devil,
to go mad so the devil will leave because
he doesn't want to be locked up with other devils.

There is the last, worst way:
coming to love the devil,
to lie in a bed, in a room
where the shades are drawn tighter than eyelids
and the body is pulled up
like a baby's fist.
Then the devil comes with his space craft.
He is the dearest one, he is the voice, he is control,
the unbroken cord that lets me float off
in that downstream of black,
tied, to the mother ship.

THE DEATH OF A REVOLUTIONARY

I, Lev, with a pick in my brain.
Me, baby Lev, undress me only you.
Natasha,
darling,
my melon, my moon.
All our children dead thanks to me.
Tasha tell, hard in the morning.
Drink tea for the revolution,
eat bread,
feed the rabbits.

It's hot in Mexico,
you are my breeze.
Funny how you...fingers cramp, crabbed...
You used to be young, why,
I love the kerchief you wear,
you, you Russian women.
Let's sleep under the bed.
You were right. His bullets
are looking out for us.

He exiled me from the snow, the dark frost,
from the cobblestones, the committees,
the lilac and the birches,
to this piace of whispers, these conspiracies of sand;
but behind the grill, behind the doors,

behind the locks, the barred windows,
behind the faithful, the calendars,
the mountains of papers, the pyramids of notes,
behind the wall of my skull
where the nerves spark connections, so necessary and true,
there, I ruled.

II

Lev, my rooster, your cockscomb dips its bloody crest.
You will die in this foreign barnyard,
your neck wrung, your skeptic eye open to the light.
His thick fingers have plucked, plucked, plucked you
in a snow of feathers.
Lev, my ikon,
I bow to you.
I bow to you.
Forgive me,
for loving our exile—
the nights of fear together—
for wanting the walls of the inner courts
for blessing the locks and the bars
that held you in for me.

STILL LIFE, BIAFRA

the head tells nothing
    bland as god.

the ribs cramp
    on emptiness

but the breasts tremble
    dark-eyed.

one hand, archaic,
    hides the sex

shriveled, withered delta
    from the metal box

soul-snatcher quick as
    the vulture's lid

open close. she is
    in this room for a little,

dense shadow. a table
    a chair, support her

not yet one of them.

LIFE AND DEATH
OF HERO STICK

God He had gone off.
Yes, He had gone.
He had shut the door.

He left us a Hero.
Yes, the Hero was left.
He was power.

Power was the stick.
Yes, it was the stick.
But Stick was afraid.

Stick was not long enough.
Stick was ashamed.
Stick hit us.

We saw Stick was small.
We said he was big.
Stick was power.

Power was Hero.
Yes, Hero was what God left us.
Hero was over us.

Stick kill little children.
Yes, our children.
Stick's children.

Stick sleep with mother.
Mother was glad.
Sticks have no eyes.

Stick kill father.
Yes, the brothers are glad.
They thank Stick.

Stick kill the brothers.
Sleep with the sisters.
They thank Stick.

We tell Stick to fight Death.
Hero puts on a dress.
Crosses the river.

The boatman fucks Stick.
Stick love it.
Not enough to be Hero.

Stick paints his mouth red.
Death feels up Stick.
Kiss me Hero.

Give me a baby, Death.
Yes, he asks Death for a baby.
Death smiles.

Show me your hole, says Death.
Stick shows his ass.
Yes, Death.

Show me another hole, says Death.
Stick opens his mouth.
Yes, Death.

I want you, Hero, says Death.
Stick cries,
I have promised my people.

How small a baby? asks Death.
As small as an egg.
As small as a bullet.

It will be a bullet, a bullet, laughs Death,
Stick, you will die.

Stick opens his mouth.
Yes, he opens.
Death shoots the bullet.

Stick spits it back.
Death sighs,
O Stick my lover, my brother,

I will not give you a baby.
You cannot kill me.
All Heroes desire me.

All Heroes become women for me.
Yes, all of them.
Yes, Death.

Take the bullet with you.
Show the people.
You are a Hero.

Come back when you are full.
Yes, Death.
Stick crosses the river.

But Death was inside him.
Stick grows fat.
I am the baby, says Death.

Yes, Death.
Stick explodes.
That is Hero's birth.

ALONE

The little voices peel off.
I'm as fragile as a woman
in a brown hat and matching coat.
Don't ask me what I do
can't you see my eyes fixed wide?
The lids can't come down.

I touched a man,
he was a burning bush.
Everyone around him
was ash ash ash.
He called to me, "mother"
and I became his wife
and worshipped his backside,
there was no other way.

When we're alone,
dark under the sheet
he was a baby at my breast
but he mouthed like a lover
when he thundered on the stage.

Men, and women, too,
he lent me to them all.
I didn't want their fingers,
I didn't want their ways.
They sent me back in taxis

marked "opened by mistake,"
so we'd crawl into bed
and have a good laugh,

until I blew up like an egg.
A baby slipped out.
Oh how he cried,
"I'm just a boy myself."
He swaggered away
down a little street.

I read him in the papers
I watch him on the news
I push around the plate the hunger
I can't eat.
And every night I ride
my pillow to sleep.

ANNE'S WEDDING

Anne stands up. I, Anne, stand up
under these trees that dispense the sun
blessing
the tables of food, and our faces.
Is this a church? There are no pews.
There are Jews, and my father's
friends, Irish to a man.
And the print-covered bosoms
murmur, "She makes a lovely bride, but
not the way it was..."

Anne, Sister Anne, I call my name.
I jilted Christ. I left him at the altar,
left him my bride's weeds.
Now I smooth my white eyelet, fondly.
Anne, Anne, I call my name,
not sure
of an answer.

Wasn't I a little girl
looking through the dust-streaked windows
at the dummy, her net veil,
her red, wooden smile?
Didn't I despise the pastel almonds
by the wedding plate,
and marriage,
the frozen horse on the stopped pole?

I took Christ to keep my self
and wonder still
what I wanted,
now I no longer want Him.

Do I choose you because your sweater
smells like my father?

I want to take the world to bed.
I want to bear the world, not bear a child.
(How long before I'll be pregnant?)
You understand? You, priest who takes a wife.
Weren't we two
afraid of becoming one,
the one that shuts the door?
There have been people, who, like trees,
nourished by the world,
gave to the world.

Family and friends,
children humming on their laps,
watch now while you and I,
a force in us like gravity,
marry.
The new verbs
tamp down the old confusions.
We receive ourselves
accepting one another.

POEM

It is morning the house sits on my chest and stares.
It is morning last night is in bed with me smiling.
It is morning the sheets whiten like notepaper.
It is morning my arms dangle, my feet refuse the floor.
It is morning, green spikey as the pines.
Quick now, the truth, whose life is it anyway?

ON REFUSING YOUR INVITATION
TO COME TO DINNER

for Cynthia

Country I've lived in, I know what I'll find:
your table,
where we will fish our reflections
from pools of polished wood;
surprise ourselves, gross
in the depths of silver spoons.

It is circumstance, not you,
the Circe I fear.
I know how the women will flicker,
beautiful as candelabra,
and twisted.
I know our eyes
staring nowhere
and our hands plucking idly at the heavy linen.
I know this terrain.

But I am forgetting the language.
Sitting has become difficult,
and the speaking, intolerable;
to say, "How interesting,"
makes me weep.
I can no longer bear to hear
the men around the table laugh,
argue, agree,
then pause politely
while we speak,

their breath held in, exhaled
when we've finished,
politely,
they turn to the real conversation,
the unspoken expectation of applause.

Once I knew their language cold.
For years I spoke it better than my own, but,
I've been away so long now, I've
grown rusty. I
stammer
take forever
to tell a story, and then
no one understands anything, except
I'm a foreigner.

And I might go beserk
after dinner, having to confront
that phalanx, wedged over brandy,
massed, to conceal the emptiness
which seeps through their ranks . . .
those strange ones, my dear,
those Ghosts-in-the-bush
who never bleed.

GREEK SONG

Quarreling, we drive over mountains
that memory will weather
to familiar monsters.
On dry slopes the bees
relate their mysteries,
but what honey can the ear harvest
from the cicada's cry?
The gold is gone
from Agamemnon's tomb;
a blackened owl
quickens within us.

Tonight, in the hotel, we lie
battening on dreams.
The pomegranate tree displays her pink
to the ripening moon.
Spurred by its light
a vine drops hearts from the balcony,
inches toward
the sound of water.

AT THE CHURCH OF THE PANAGIA KERA
(ALL HOLY LADY)

Wind drums through fallen stones. Here
it hums like the German tourist
inspecting the frescoes
where the Holy Fathers glower,
pinched nostrils
scenting heresy in our presence.

Peering from the chapel with her raccoon eyes
the Madonna reveals her disapproval
of the men who usurped her power,
murdered her son.

Mildew has damped the Byzantine fires,
and the sacred comics go unread,
but outside, plaster maintains a candor
white enough to slash the eye.

In the groves nearby,
wimpled women on donkeys
ride over a bloody clay.
Under black rags their bodies droop
like Hers: marriage, rape, abortions, births
burials . . . the Old Religion.

Passing, they nod,
offer us grapes. They own this land,

strength in those hands
whose touch is dry and quick as snakes.

They move on
towards the mountains
and caves
where they have always adored
the Holy She.

There is no ceremony they are not ready for.

PERSEPHONE DEPARTS

Merely turning her back,
she goes
down the street.

I shut the windows against the rains,
keeping indoors, ravished,
like the great maple out there,
diminishing,
remembering all things shared—
all but her dark longings
that pulled her from me,
just as earth
tugs at the swollen pear.

She goes
farther than I would have borne her:
out of reach of my dreams. Now
in these haunted rooms
my rage whips the bare, stripped world,
I wheel, the sky closed down,
eclipsed.

INITIATION

for Harriet

I comb your hair.

(Under the birches stained red
the women
are weaving a robe.)

You pull away. Your back slams a door.
From the other side
you clamor, "Love me."

(Bone chorus
dancing the songs
of change)

Your hair spreads like the grass.
"What you said to me
was cruel, mother."

(Shadows from the grove
drawing near)

The teeth of the comb drag.
My shorn head bends, intent
on your instruction.

SHE PAINTS

The children, now, she remembers
soft and young, hanging
from her like peaches;

of the husband less:
the razor on the washstand
the wedding shoes on the cold feet.

In the glare of noon she explodes
at the window. Flowers
clot at the garden wall.

Color splinters her eyes,
her hands are two
unknown maps.

Brushes work the canvas—
shapes swell
clustered like grapes, like bee cells.

She paints mother as saint,
father as bull, the baby
smooth as a soapy Jesus.

Paints the denial of years,
lead white of grub,
arteries of trees.

Paints Love going by
with his swollen neck,
his red slit eye.

At her ear voices whisper.
She grows afraid. Fear
sheets the visions.

The cicada's hollow casing
glints at the foot
of the pines.

Rocks press on her,
roots caress her face
dark and quiet.

Cunning as a hand
reaching from a corner,
she paints out the light until

mouth fills with brown,
eyes with brown, ears stopped
the heart runs down in brown,

and death is two black pennies
on her eyes.

VOYAGES

Who was I
when I took the nipple,
floating through space,
when the big shadow
out of focus
rocked me and watched?

Who was I
when the moons stood round,
tightness in my throat,
trembling under new hands?

Who lay on a table flung open,
the "no" faces nodding?
Pain was a pulse of flight
firing me to the stars,
the pod burst,
the years streamed by,
a body in the breath, struggling.

Where have I arrived now?
What is this thing, "growing old"?
Monstrous, how I am held:
its skin speaking to my skin
it coming into my dark
it telling me I will forget.

Someone is crying in this place.
The waters break over my head.

WAKING

My body under you, like a mine field,
a white light seeds us into stone;
hour when only a fool wakes to find
the intruder going through his pockets,
stealing his lies.

Here are the things we never say,
laid out like a well-thumbed deck.
Swords, swords, no matter how I deal.

Kristallnacht, morning will cut her wrists
on your clarities.
I was born to die of truth, taking you
with me.

ALL HALLOWS' EVE

They rise tonight the dead,
who know of us
all we fear to have discovered;
the unforgiveable dead
with their irrevocable conclusions.

And the still unsettled dead
rise, too, and stand
outside our doors,
rehearsing the terrible question.

Imperative, they whisper
"You are loved."
Trembling, they poise
attentive to our wishes, ready
to fall under the wheel.

Ancestor figures, nailed to our granary doors
in times of plenty, in times of dearth,
they move tonight—O Master of Masks—
calling us forth to inhabit us,
to harness our lives, to ride us like the tides.

SHE COMES TO HIM
ON THEIR ANNIVERSARY

Gloves tossed away,
open, rapturous, empty hands.
Water glass by the bed.
Something old at last broken.
Something new, at last, joined.
The bridle is worn,
the land bows its neck, gleaming.

THE SOLITARY ONE

For so long the ground was worked,
then, growth bestowed itself,
not as recompense, but
generosity.

Cactus
with your aureole of spines,
only the air
dares embrace you.

DATE DUE

7/29/08			

#47-0108 Peel Off Pressure Sensitive